Interpreting, Understanding, and Managing the Numbers

Financial Intelligence for IT Managers

By Thomas Markham and James Wilson

Table of Contents

Table of Figures

Topic 1: Setting a Baseline for Learning the Numbers

Why are there challenges to learning accounting and finance?

Often, students who try to learn accounting and finance will often say they are "not good at math". However, this is a myth and really does not address the underlying issue of why this topic is challenging.

There are a few reasons why learning about the world of numbers in a business can be a difficult endeavor, so let us go through them so you can dispel the myth that finance and accounting are hard.

Terminology can be tricky.

Terminology is not standard in the world of accounting and finance. For example, when you are learning about an income statement, there is no standard template for how accounts are named. Thus, when you are learning about Revenue, this can also be called Net Revenue, Total Sales,

Net Sales, or Sales Revenue. Or, the Cost of Goods Sold could be called Cost of Revenue. Thus, when you are learning this field, you have to be aware of the fact and check to see if this is the learning barrier. If it is, ask for clarification.

Terminology drives the math.

In the world of accounting and finance, if you do not understand the terminology, then you will have challenges with the math. For example, most people have heard of the term "depreciation", because we all have cars and we know the car depreciates in value over time. In accounting terms, knowing that accounting rules have specific processes for accounting for depreciation is important to know. Thus, if you have the contextual framework for this accounting treatment, then the math should be easier to apply. In addition, depreciation is a non-cash expenditure. Therefore, in a lot of the internal modeling for looking at return on investment, depreciation has special treatment and consideration in those models because it is a non-cash expense.

Your teacher/mentor needs to build pathways in your brain.

Since terminology can create issues for a student's learning, having a teacher or a mentor that can help you build the mental pathways on how to THINK about accounting, you will have a much higher likelihood to learn what is necessary for you to be financially intelligent.

Generally, what this means is that to learn a concept, you need the background, or the context of what you are learning, to then see an explained example of the application, and then your own practice. Ultimately, you will need to work with financial information on a regular basis to get it down and what this may mean is finding a good teacher and that may be a mentor in your accounting department!

Why is it important to learn financial intelligence/literacy?

In terms of a career path, learning about finance and accounting as you move up the ranks is important. At any time, you could be managing a budget and having to explain variances, or you may have to put together an IT department capital investment plan, or you could have to justify a large investment into computer hardware or software.

However, there is an even more important reason. As an employee of an organization, it behooves you to understand some basics of accounting and finance because you want to understand how the company is performing, financially, by doing your OWN analysis and not relying on others to tell you how the company is doing.

Would you be able to see if a company is poorly performing or bleeding money? Later on in the book we will take a look at a company that went into bankruptcy and you will be able to see just how bad the clash flow was and that it should have been a sign to employees of the company tanking. When you can spot these signs yourself, you are then empowered to make your own decisions for your financial future.

Other challenges.

In the world of company finance and accounting (or financial accounting), we will talk about the fact that publicly traded companies have to file external reporting for their stockholders and those who may want to invest in the company. The format of these documents is fairly standard, but some accounts can be called different things., i.e., revenue can be called sales, among other challenges.

However, when we talk about internal reporting and modeling, the domain that is generally called managerial accounting, the standards get even murkier. Every company can produce their own return on investments models, based on how they want to approach assessing projects and investments. Variance calculations can be pretty standard but a lot of analysis internally to an organization is often housed in Excel and the models are determined by those who build them. Thus, often times, one model does not fit all, or one approach does not fit all – much will depend on your staff/leadership and your industry.

How this book is helps address these challenges.

In this book, we will walk through analyzing two technology organizations, Amazon (AMZN) and Google (GOOG). As we walk through each company and their financial information, we will be highlighting the concepts and framework for how to interpret their financial information.

In addition, we will highlight what each topic means to a person that starts a technology company, works for a technology company, or works in an information technology department.

We will also go through calculation in detail, explaining the what, how, and why of the calculations. Each topic will be support by video explanations, as well, in order to help visual learners.

Finally, there are some topics that will not be addressed by static "models". Instead, you will be taught how to think about a model, but you would eventually have to design your own model. However, it is important that you learn the thought process behind building a model so that you can then design your own model with clarity.

For individuals who would like to use this as a workbook, you can download the source documents used in this book:

Google Financials: http://bit.ly/Google10k

Amazon Financials: http://bit.ly/Amazon10-k

It is highly recommended that you download these 10-k reports so that you can follow along with the calculations and so you can see where the source data is coming from throughout the book. In addition, it is highly recommended that you periodically read sections of the reports. One of the important things to do is to make sure that you understand how a company operates. One of the problems Enron had is that analysts and reporters sometimes had challenges understanding how the company made money.

You should never invest or work for a company that you cannot understand how they make money.

Now, it is likely there will be certain concepts in a 10-k that you may not understand right away. It is important to utilize the expertise of your accounting resources to make sure that you understand key financial topics. If, within a brief period of time, you are not able to understand a topic, then that should be a red flag for you as well.

The most important goal is to educate yourself. Own the interpretation and understanding of financial information for yourself. As a future business owner, or as an employee, you do not want to be in a position to lose your life savings like Enron employees did.

Even better, if you are currently working for a company, use their financial statements!

Topic 2: Income Statement - Revenue

What is a fiscal year?

Before discussing any of the financial statements, not every business has a fiscal year that ends on December 31. It just so happens that for Amazon and for Google the fiscal year does end on December 31. However, for financial reporting at most retail organizations, their fiscal year ends are NOT on December 31. Thus, you want to be clear on what period the fiscal, or financial, year represents for any organization that you study.

What is an income statement?

An income statement shows the revenue and expenses of an organization. The income statement can also be called "profit and loss statement", or just "P&L". The Income statement will cover a period of time, usually a month, and it will actually state "for the period of ___". In this first topic, we will focus on the first line of every income statement: REVENUE (or Sales).

What is revenue?

Revenue represents the sales of any company. Depending on the organization, sales can represent a lot of different things, so we want to go into some detail, using Amazon as an example, to explore sales for a technology-oriented organization.

What is revenue recognition?

For an information technology (IT) department in an organization where information technology is not the business model, you would be concerned about revenue when you are supporting a sales department. However, if you are an information technology business, you will want to consider how revenue and cash flow through your business model.

There are nuances to when revenue is recognized versus when cash is received. We will be exploring revenue recognition and unearned revenue and demonstrating how cash flows through an organization based on these principles.

First, how do you figure out how a company makes money? One of the best ways to find this out is to pull the 10-k report from a company's website. In this case, we have pulled the 10-K for 2018 for Amazon from the corporate website at amazon.com. Traditionally, you will find this by going to the company website and looking for a section called "Investor Relations", or you can go to the Securities and Exchange Commission (www.sec.gov). You will see a search function and underneath that you will see "company filings". Click on company filings, then enter a company name and click "search". Then look for the 10-k for a specific year.

A 10-k is required to be published if a company is publicly traded. If a company is privately owned, there is no requirement to file with the Securities and Exchange Commission. If you work for a company that is not publicly traded, then hopefully your company is transparent with financial statements and you can get your hands on them to do this analysis.

Now, to find out how a company makes money, you can do word searches in the PDF document. To do a word search in a PDF file, you can use "CTRL-F" and then type in the terms you want to find. If you search for "revenue" in the 2018 10-k for Amazon, you will find information about seasonality, "Our business is affected by seasonality, which historically has resulted in higher sales volume during our fourth quarter, which ends December 31" (page 4). Amazon does not explain this any more than that, but we can deduce that because of the holidays, the seasonality is common in their sales around the holidays.

If you keep searching for "revenue", you will eventually get to Page 28 of the 10-k, that states, "Net sales include product and service sales. Product sales represent revenue from the sale of products and related shipping fees and digital media content...[sic]...Service sales primarily represent third party seller fees,...AWS sales, Amazon

Prime membership fees, advertising services and certain digital content subscriptions."

In addition, if you look at page 42 of the Amazon 10-k for 2018, you see that revenue recognition occurs when ownership changes hands (i.e., when product is delivered to the customer) or the revenue is recognized over the life a subscription (i.e., the Prime membership is recognized over the life of the subscription).

Why does revenue NOT always equal cash?

It may be surprising to you that revenue does not qual cash, but there is a reason for this phenomenon. For instance, revenue and cash may occur at different points in time. Thus, it is important to understand this from the standpoint of illustrating how the Amazon Prime Membership works in terms of revenue and the receipt of cash.

Example: Amazon Prime Memberships: First, take Amazon Prime memberships. For ease of math, assume an Amazon Prime membership is $120 per year. When a consumer purchases a Prime membership, they are paying UP FRONT for a year's worth of services. In addition, consumers pay for the services on a credit card; therefore, Amazon gets all the cash upfront as well.

However, Amazon is not allowed by Generally Accepted Accounting Principles (GAAP – these are the rules/guidelines that accountants have to abide by) to recognize the entire $120 as revenue when the consumer buys the service. Instead, Amazon can only recognize $1/12^{th}$ of the Amazon Prime membership each month, for the next twelve months.

MONTHS	May	Jun	Jul	Aug	Sep	Oct	Nov	Dec	Jan	Feb	Mar	Apr
CASH	$120.00											
REVENUE	$ 12.00	$12.00	$12.00	$12.00	$12.00	$12.00	$12.00	$12.00	$12.00	$12.00	$12.00	$12.00

Figure 1 Example of an Amazon Prime Membership

For example, in Figure 1 above, you can see a consumer purchased the membership in May, and all the cash is received in May, but the revenue will be spread out over twelve months. Likewise, if a Prime membership is sold in

November, the income statement would reflect income for November and December, and then the rest of the revenue will be recognized the next year.

Not all revenue is recognized like this, however any type of subscription should be treated this way. Amazon has monthly billing for Amazon Web Services. It is not clear if the company always bills that on a credit card, but it may be a combination of charging a credit card or invoicing clients. When a customer is invoice, revenue is recognized at the time of invoicing. If a client is billed then by credit card, cash comes into Amazon within 24-48 hours. If a client is being billed, with terms like 30 days, the cash will come into the bank usually within 30 days.

From just this level of an examination of Amazon, you can see that the cash flow from sales is good. The timing of the cash flow is often coming in before the revenue must be recognized. Later, you will see why this cash flow process of a technology company is well rewarded on stock exchanges.

What is different in a small business?

A small business will also have an income statement; however, a small business will not be required to send financial information to the Securities and Exchange Commission.

One small business has developed an add-on to PowerPoint using Excel functionality so that a user can create timelines, like Gantt charts, in PowerPoint. The company sells this product for a year's subscription for $59.

Since they do not report information to the Securities and Exchange Commission, they have been recognizing all that revenue at the time the customer pays. However, the company is starting to think about moving towards recognition of revenue over the year. The company leadership is starting to think about what is necessary if the company were to be acquired by another organization.

Furthermore, a company, if it is not publicly traded, can follow a cash basis of accounting. Thus, if this small business receives $59 for a subscription, then they can report that $59 in the month it was received because cash flowed into the bank account at the bank. If the small business wants to be attractive to a potential merger or acquisition by another company, then the small business must think about how to move towards the rules that a publicly traded company must follow (if the merging or acquiring company is publicly traded).

In the case of this small business, this is the only product line it has, and the product is digital, and subscription based.

Implications for your learning:

1. Understand how revenue is recognized for your product lines
2. Understand how cash is generated from your product lines (if cash is received before goods and

services are exchanged, at the same time goods and services are exchanged, or cash is received after goods and services are exchanged)

3. Understand that profit/revenue does not necessarily equal cash in the bank

4. In an IT department, you may be supporting point of sales systems.

5. While the IT department most likely will not be generating sales, you could be developing an application that captures sales

6. Understanding about the business model of your company, only aids your growth into higher levels of responsibility and promotion

Topic 3: Income Statement – Cost of Goods Sold

The next item on an income statement is cost of goods sold, and this can also be called cost of revenue or cost of sales. Depending on what source you pull an income statement from this item can be called different things.

What are Cost of Goods Sold?

Cost of goods sold represents the cost that are incurred in generating a sale.

Why is cost of goods an estimate?

Costs of products are easily traced to the finished product or they may not be easily traceable to the finished product. For instance, if Amazon produces the Kindle, there is a motherboard and there is a microphone. These parts of a Kindle are easily traceable to the production of a Kindle. However, if there is a machine that puts some parts together on an assembly line, or if there are people that have to do certain tasks associated with the assembly, it would be much harder to trace those costs. It is likely that

Amazon may not produce this product, they may have a production agreement with a manufacturer, and thus Amazon may actually be an exclusive reseller of a Kindle product. The 10-k for Amazon did not directly address this specific question.

For instance, a company could be a merchandiser, or reseller, of goods. In this case, a company would buy products at a lower cost and then resell them at a marked-up price. In this situation it could be easier to trace the costs directly to the sale, but it may not be easy at all.

In another company, they may manufacture products. In this case, in a manufacturing facility, there can be a lot of expensive machinery and the depreciation is an overhead cost. But how do you apply that cost to one product? Can you trace overhead to one sole product? No. Thus, a company, when pricing those products and determining the cost of the product must have some method by which they apply overhead to a product. Maybe it is based on production units, or it is based on labor hours, either way, it is not an exact science.

Now, in the 10-k, you cannot find information about the base cost to manufacture a Kindle, but if you google the base price of a Kindle, you can find information from some reputable sources that Amazon may take a small loss on the sale of every Kindle. The speculation is that Amazon feels like a small loss on the product is worthwhile, especially if Amazon can get a user to subscribe to Kindle content. Remember, a subscription model is a great way to have continuous income, thus it may be very advantageous for a one-time product to be sold at a loss if the long-term revenue of a subscription is factored into the equation.

Consider the math. If Amazon loses $5 on the sale of a Kindle, but a subscriber signs up for $9.99 a month for a subscription, the loss will be more than covered. Not every person that buys a Kindle will go with a Kindle subscription, but the company probably knows (internally) if this is a winning strategy. The accountants and financial officers should keep an eye on this to ensure that the small loss is worth it!

Are there timing issues with cost of goods and cash?

Yes! Let us say that Amazon buys the Kindle from an exclusive partnership with a manufacturer. We will assume that ownership for that product may switch from the manufacturer to Amazon at the time the product is loaded onto a truck at the manufacturer's warehouse. At the same time, the manufacturer most likely will invoice Amazon for the total purchase cost. We will assume that Amazon has 30 days to pay that invoice.

From the date that the product is shipped, cash will be exchanged within 30 days of that event.

However, products may still be sitting in inventory, waiting to be sold, after that initial 30 days. Only when the product is sold will Amazon recognize the cost of the product. But the cash has most likely been spent on the product before the sale ever occurs.

Why should you care about product costs versus operating costs?

Product costs are associated with a product sale. Thus, if you have no sales, you will have product sitting in your inventory waiting to be sold.

Operating costs are in a separate section of the income statement. These are ongoing costs that a business incurs regardless of whether a sale happens or not. For example, if a business is paying rent on space, that expense will occur no matter how much revenue is generated.

In fact, a business owner asked once "what does it cost me to run my business"? The answer to that is your operating costs. If you look at the "Consolidated Statements of Operations" in the 10-k for Amazon (another way of saying "Income Statement") you will see that Amazon includes cost of sales in the operating expenses. However, if you look at finance.yahoo.com and pull up Amazon financials, the cost of sales is placed in the cost of goods sold spot on the income statement.

Typically, for analysis purposes, you would see cost of sales directly related to the revenue, but this just goes to show you that there is no standard presentation of an income statement. Your goal, as a student of financial literacy, is to understand when these things are of concern and when they are not a concern.

This should not be a concern. However, later on when we discuss analyzing a company from a ratio perspective, this will be an important concept to revisit.

What is different in a small technology business?

Not much is different between a publicly traded business versus a small business. The big difference may lie in the fact that a company that is not publicly traded can produce income statements that are bank account/checking account centered. Meaning that as the money comes in and out of the business, that is when costs are recorded on the income statement. Therefore, if a small business had an exclusive manufacturing relationship and purchased product, all that product cost might be represented in the income statement all at once and not sit in inventory on the balance sheet like a publicly traded company.

In the case of the small business that has a digital add on to PowerPoint, their direct cost of sales includes credit card processing fees. However, the company also has a product development team in another country. This product development team does many things – make enhancements to the digital product, they establish marketing platforms and maintain the website presence, they do all the digital marketing on Facebook, Google and other platforms. At this time, that company has not broken apart support functions and development functions, but they have a unique challenge in being able to trace direct costs to that digital product. Thus, the company could consider all of the development costs as a cost of sales, but right now, like Amazon, they include these costs in their operating costs. Later, when we look at ratios, we will demonstrate how this small company compares to Amazon and we will consider those costs as "cost of sales" so there will be an "apple to apples" comparison.

Implications for your learning:

1. Understand how cost of goods sold is estimated in your organization, the estimate may be small, or they may be a lot. Knowing how much they are estimated is key

2. Operating costs are the costs of running your business – regardless of how much your sell or do not sell

3. If you run a small business, it is important to note that if a company ever considers acquiring your business, cost of goods sold will be an important conversation to have about what encompasses that number. For a lot of information technology businesses – this is the direct development costs.

4. On an income statement, "cost of goods sold" could also be called "cost of revenue" – so do not be confused!

Topic 4: Income Statement – Gross Profit

On a typical income statement, after REVENUE and COST OF GOODS SOLD you will have a GROSS PROFIT. Gros Profit is a calculated number where you take the Revenue minus the Cost of Goods Sold to derive the Gross Profit number.

Gross profit represented the cents, per dollar, that you have been able to retain in the business to cover your operating and other costs.

How do you calculate gross profit margin?

One of the ratios that you can use to assess profitability is the gross profit margin (a percentage). To calculate this ratio, you would take the Gross Profit and divide it by the Revenue.

$$\frac{\text{Gross Profit}}{\text{Revenue}}$$

Figure 2 Gross Profit Margin Calculation

Be aware that if you search the web for videos on this subject, you will find that some people use this formula:

$$\frac{\text{Revenue - Cost of Goods Sold}}{\text{Revenue}}$$

Figure 3 Alternate Calculation Gross Profit Margin

Be advised that Revenue – Cost of Goods Sold does equal gross profit, which is the numerator in the original formula. Thus, the sources are talking about the exact same thing!

Below, you can view a video about this calculation (http://bit.ly/V1-1)

Figure 4 Gross Profit Margin Calculation Video

Using this formula, here are the calculations for Amazon:

	Amazon (AMZN)				
		Numbers are in millions			
	2018		2017		2016
$	93,731.00	$	65,932.00	$	47,722.00
$	232,887.00	$	177,866.00	$	135,987.00
	0.40		0.37		0.35

Figure 5 Gross Profit Calculation for Amazon

Before getting into these results, please notice that these numbers are represented in "millions". Thus, in 2018, the number we have in the formula for revenue is $232,887. You would tend to think this is thousands of dollars; however, you must add on six additional zeros for the true number. Thus, this is over $232 BILLION dollars in revenue. When you look at a source for a financial statement, you want to be sure and look at how the number is represented.

In addition, these numbers come from the "Consolidated Statements of Operations" (Amazon does not even call it an income statement or profit and loss) on page 37 of the Amazon 10-k. The $232,887 number is the "Total net sales" for 2018. You have to "back into" the gross profit. You have to take the $232,887 and subtract from that the

"Cost of Sales" of $139,156 to arrive at $93,731. You will do the same calculations for 2017 and 2016. The important thing to learn here is that the income statements has revenue, costs of goods sold, operating expenses, and net income/loss, but how this is presented can look different by company.

So, what do these numbers tell us about Amazon's financial performance? Think of these numbers in this manner: in 2015, Amazon was able to keep 33 cents from every $1 of sales. By 2018, Amazon has improved this number to 40 cents of every $1 of sales.

The next question is how good or bad is this? The answer is that we have to compare Amazon to a competitor in order to judge how this performance stacks up. Also bear in mind that often, even companies in the same industry are not exactly alike. But let us consider Google (GOOG).

	Google (GOOG)				
	Numbers are in millions				
	2018		2017		2016
$	77,270.00	$	65,273.00	$	55,134.00
$	136,819.00	$	110,855.00	$	90,272.00
	0.56		0.59		0.61

Figure 6 Gross Profit Calculation for Google

These numbers are found on the Google 10-k by looking at the "Consolidated Statements of Income" on page 47. For Google, in 2018, the top line "Revenues" is $136,819. But similar to Amazon, you have to "back into" the gross profit. You take the revenue of $136,819 and subtract the "cost of revenues" of $59,549 to arrive at a gross profit of $77,270. The same calculation would be done for 2017 and 2016.

By contrast, Google is consistently generating a gross profit of around 58 cents per $1 of sales. This is quite different than Amazon. There could be many reasons for this. As you examine the financial statements, news articles and the 10-k report for these companies, you may find more examples of loss leader items at Amazon. Maybe that is the reason their margin is not higher. Ultimately, studying the company financial information, even if not all of it makes sense, the more you read, the more you practice, the better you will get at understanding these numbers for any company.

What is a good target gross profit margin for a business?

The answer to this question is somewhat murky. The answer will depend on your industry, for example. Technology company tend to have higher gross margins, restaurants tend to have lower gross margins. Generally speaking, if your gross profit margins are consistently around 15-20%, you could easily be impacted in economic downturns. You can see this often play out in the restaurant industry. For instance, when there are major market corrections or big economic downturns like the financial collapse in 2008-2009, many restaurants went out of business. That would make sense, intuitively, because the restaurant industry, to a consumer, is often a discretionary expense. When the purse strings tighten, it is easy to cut out going out to lunch or dinner.

One way that restaurants can counterbalance this potential economic risk is to promote the use of gift cards. Gift cards are one of those instruments that enables an organization to obtain an influx of cash, before revenue must be recognized. From a cash flow perspective, this strategy can certainly help keep a business afloat.

It is important then to be a keen observer of companies that interest you, either as an investor, or as an employee. By understanding the business model and how the business model impacts the numbers, you can be more empowered.

Implications for a technology company/startup:

For a technology company or startup, paying attention to the gross profit will set the tone for the financial success of the company. Having a healthy gross profit gives you room for your operating costs. Since a lot of technology can be cloud based today, or digital, gross profits in a technology organization can be healthy, in the 50% or greater category.

Implications for your learning:

1. Know your company's gross profit margin

2. Even an IT department staff should know this number and why it matters to everyone

3. IT businesses, in general, tend to have healthy gross profit margins

4. You can calculate gross profit margins on different departments of your business and different product lines

5. Be aware that gross profit may not appear as a separate line on an income statement – you may have to "back into" that number

6. Also be aware that the financial statement may be called "operations", "income", or "profit and loss". Just remember you are looking for revenues, cost of goods sold, etc., to know when you have found the right statement

Topic 5: Income Statement – Operating Costs

After Gross Profit on an Income Statement you will see operating costs. Generally, the account you will often see here that has the largest amount of dollars in it is an account called "Selling, General and Administrative" costs. Sometimes you will hear this called by an acronym of "SG&A".

What is in SG&A?

These general expenses can include rent payments, utilities costs, salaries of support function personnel (i.e., legal departments, IT departments, accounting departments, sales, and marketing teams, etc.).

What timing issues exist in Operating Expenses?

You have learned, in previous topics, that profit does not equal cash. This is because there are often timing issues of cash being generated or used versus when it is recorded on the financial statements. This is true in operating expenses as well. Here are some examples:

1. Depreciation

Depreciation is an approved accounting methodology that gives a company a way of estimating the value of an asset over time. Just like when you buy a car, you can check the Kelly Blue Book value of that car, at any point in the car's lifecycle, to get an idea of the value.

A company can take an asset (a building, a piece of machinery, or a capital expenditure in Information Technology) and depreciate that asset over time. This is an approved deduction that can be created in operating expenses and thus reduces the amount of net income a company can have in any given period.

Essentially, this is a business deduction, and the cash is not actually paid to anyone. This cash stays in house. No check is written to any government agency. Thus, buried in the SG&A expenses are accounts that have to do with depreciation expense.

We can find out how much a company has "spent", or deducted, in depreciation expense on the cash flow statement. Here are the numbers for Amazon (AMZN):

Amazon (in millions)	
2018	$ 15,341.00
2017	$ 11,478.00
2016	$ 8,116.00
2015	$ 5,646.00

Figure 7 Amazon Depreciation Yearly Expense

Another way to look at it is this: In 2018 Amazon (AMZN) reported a net income of $10,073. However, that number EXCLUDES the depreciation expense (and that expense never was paid to any organization). Essentially, the TRUE net income for Amazon (AMZN) in 2018 was $10,073 PLUS $15,341 for an amount of $25,414 (that is 25 billion dollars – because the numbers are expressed in millions – meaning all numbers will have SIX zeros added to them).

Another way this is discussed among financial experts is the EBITDA (which stands for the Earnings Before

Interest, Tax, Depreciation and Amortization. This is commonly shown on the income statement as the operating income line, which is $12,421 for Amazon in 2018, and then you add back in depreciation of $15,341 and you have $27,762.

2. Matching expenses to the period

One of the rules that accountants have to live by is matching expenses to the correct period. One example of this is often salary expenses. Consider the following scenario.

Assume that you have employees that are paid every Friday and the weekly pay is $5,000. In addition, assume that at the end of December the last Friday of the month is December 27. The next payday will be January 3rd of the next year. Thus, there are a couple of days, December 30, and December 31 where the company will have to recognize salary expense even though the expenses have not actually been paid yet. This is known as an accrual of expense, so that the expenses appear is the right reporting period of December.

One method for doing this is that if the company works a five-day week, then the $5,000 in salary expense could be divided by 5 days. Thus, $5,000 / 5 days would be $1,000 of salary expense per day. If you are then accruing for two days of salary expense, the accrual would be for $2,000 ($1,000 per day times 2).

3. Prepaid Expenses

Your company may be one that has good cash flow and you may choose to prepay expenses. An example may be paying your health insurance benefits for the whole year in order to get a substantial discount.

Consider a scenario where you may have health benefits that cost $6,000 for the year. Since a company should only recognize expenses in the period that they should be recognized, it is not a good idea to expense the entire $6,000 in one month on your profit and loss. Instead, if you follow the rules, you would only recognize $500 each month. Thus, $500 times 12 = $6,000.

In this case, you would be paying out $6,000 in cash, but you would home that amount on the balance sheet in a prepaid expense account and you would expense $500 each month until the balance sheet amount is exhausted.

What does this mean to you as an IT manager?

From these examples, you can see that expenses can be in your department budgets that may not have been paid. If you see your budgets fluctuating a lot, you may want to talk with your accounting support about what the source of the fluctuation. Now, it may be that it is a certain time of increased projects for your staff, or it may be an unusual set of expenses hitting your budget. However, you should have an idea of what drives your costs and when these costs are not behaving as expected.

What does this mean to you as a technology startup?

If you are not a publicly traded company, then you do not necessarily have to follow the rules of matching. Thus, you would be most likely following a cash basis of accounting. However, if you are successful as a technology startup, there could come a day when you could be considered as an acquisition by another company. If that is the case, the acquiring company will likely expect that the financial statements are prepared in accordance to these rules.

Implications for your learning:

1. Depreciation is a non-cash expense
2. The matching principle requires recognizing expenses even if they have not been paid in the current period
3. Timing is a crucial learning element when trying to figure out how cash is flowing in a company

Topic 6: Income Statement – Net Income

What is Net Income?

Net income is the *estimated* amount of income that a company has generated each reporting period. Net income is the bottom-line net profit or loss of a company; however, remember it is an estimated net profit.

One way of seeing how the net income performs over time, we can approach this with a similar computation that we did for gross profit.

In Topic 4 we discussed gross profit margin and now we will do a similar calculation called net profit margin to assess profitability. To make this calculation we will take the net income number and divide by revenue. Here is the formula:

$$\frac{\text{Net Profit}}{\text{Revenue}}$$

Figure 8 Net Profit Margin Calculation

You can use the following video to learn about calculating net profit margin as a ratio (http://bit.ly/V1-2)

Figure 9 Net Profit Margin Calculation Video

In using this formula, we can then calculate the net profit margin. For Google, the data shows:

	Google (GOOG) Numbers are in millions				
	2018		2017		2016
$	30,736.00	$	12,662.00	$	19,478.00
$	136,819.00	$	110,855.00	$	90,272.00
	0.22		0.11		0.22

Figure 10 Google Net Profit Margin Calculation

The information for this calculation comes from the income statement. For Google, you find the information on the "Consolidated Statements of Income" on page 47. For 2018, for example, the revenue number is from the very top line of the statement for 2018 of $136,819. The net income number is at the bottom for 2018 of $30,736. For 2017 and 2016 you would pull the data from the same spots.

This shows us that Google kept an estimated 22 cents of every dollar in 2018 as their bottom-line net profit/income. Compared to 11 cents in 2017 and 22 cents in 2016.

The trend we see with Google is that the net profit margin dropped in 2017. In the 10-k, Google explains that the drop was because of a charge related to the Tax Cuts and Jobs Act.

Then we turn to Amazon to see their results:

Amazon (AMZN)					
Numbers are in millions					
2018		2017		2016	
$	10,073.00	$	3,033.00	$	2,371.00
$	232,887.00	$	177,866.00	$	135,987.00
	0.04		0.02		0.02

Figure 11 Amazon Net Profit Margin Calculation

For Amazon, you will pull these numbers from the "Consolidated Statements of Operations" on page 37. For 2018, the revenue number is the "total net sales" of the statement of $232,887 and the net income is at the bottom on the net income line of $10,073.

Here we see a consistent net profit margin. In 2018, Amazon kept an estimated 4 cents of every dollar generated in revenue as their net bottom line.

Implications for your learning:

1. Net income is an estimated number
2. **Even though net income is estimated, the ratio should be consistent over time**

Topic 7: Balance Sheet – Assets

A balance sheet is repository of all of the financial decisions made over time by a company. A balance sheet will be produced at a point in time, thus the balance sheet will say "as of _____" and the date the balance sheet was produced.

What are assets?

For any company, assets are anything that has a cash value or anything that can help a company make sales. Further, if you look on the balance sheet, assets can be considered "current" (meaning, you can turn them into cash in a year or less), or "long term" assets, which help a company to create cash over a period longer than a year.

Working Capital:

When someone refers to working capital, they are referring to the current assets of the business and how those assets are being managed to turn them into cash.

For sake of this conversation, cash is already cash, there is no need to be concerned about converting that asset to cash because it is the cash that the business has on hand. Cash equivalents are usually securities that can be converted to cash very quickly, usually within hours and all it takes is going to the bank or a brokerage site to make that transaction happen.

Thus, what we are talking about in working capital management is how quickly we can convert accounts receivable and inventory into cash. These conversions require customers to engage with us, to pay invoice they owe and to buy product from us. Therefore, we must have strategies on how to minimize how long an invoice stays open or how long inventory stays on the shelf.

Cash:

Cash is the asset that is most liquid. Liquidity means that an asset can be turned into cash quickly. Cash is already cash, so that is why it is listed FIRST on the balance sheet in the Current Assets section.

Accounts Receivable:

Generally, with accounts receivable, someone needs to keep their eye on the "aging" of invoices. Depending on the size of a company, you will need the ability to be able to see reporting on your invoices by invoice number, by customer, by sales department, or any other criteria that is meaningful to your business. This ONLY matters to you if your business invoices customers. If you are direct billing a credit card, you have other potential issues you may need to address but converting receivables would not be one of the issues.

According to the 10-k of Amazon, if you search on "accounts receivable" you find on 45 that "customer receivables, net, were $6.4 billion". They have some other types of receivables as well that are unique to Amazon.

Right underneath that paragraph is a paragraph that also gives us a clue as to how much of that $6.4 billion is at risk for being written off or being sent to a collection agency.

According to the 10-k, page 45, the "allowance for doubtful accounts was $237 million" (we are assuming that the first number aligns with the first number in the paragraph preceding it and that this number aligns to the customer receivables).

Current Ratio:

The current ratio is a ratio that assesses the liquidity of a company. Liquidity means that you are able to pay your bills in the short-term.

Here is the calculation for the current ratio:

$$\frac{\text{Current Assets}}{\text{Current Liabilities}}$$

Figure 12 The Current Ratio Calculation

The current ratio target is for the result to be great than 1 on a consistent basis. Think about why that is – if we have a current ratio result of 1, then our current assets are equaling our current liabilities. If the result is LESS THAN 1, then that means our current BILLS are greater than the resources we have to pay those bills. If we stay in that kind of position, then it could become hard to pay our bills at some point in the future, which will show a potential cash flow issue.

However, if our result is GREATER THAN 1, then we have plenty of cash, or the potential to generate cash, to cover our current bills.

For further information, here is a video to help explain the current ratio (http://bit.ly/V1-3)

Figure 13 Video on Current Ratio

Now, let us take a look at how this ratio works for Amazon:

Amazon (AMZN)		
Numbers are in millions		
2018		2017
$ 75,101.00	$	60,197.00
$ 68,391.00	$	57,883.00
1.10		1.04

Figure 14 Current Ratio Calculation for Amazon

The information for this calculation is pulled from the balance sheet. For Amazon, the statement you are looking for is the "Consolidated Balance Sheets" on page 39. In 2018, you are looking for the "Total current assets" line of $75,101 and the "Total current liabilities" of $68,391. You will use the same lines for the 2017 calculation.

Amazon looks good, with a 1.10 current ratio for 2018 and a 1.04 current ratio for 2017, but now you should compare the information to Google:

Google (GOOG)		
Numbers are in millions		
2018		2017
$ 135,676.00	$	124,308.00
$ 34,620.00	$	24,183.00
3.92		5.14

Figure 15 Current Ratio Calculation for Google

For Google, you will look at the "Consolidated Balance Sheets" on Page 46. For 2018, you will pull the "Total current assets" of $135,676 and the "Total current liabilities" of $34,620. You will use the same lines of the statement for pulling data for 2017.

They both are doing well in the current ratio; however, Google is showing a more comfortable position. Google is showing a healthy current ratio of 3.92 in 2018, and a current ratio of 5.14 in 2017.

Quick Ratio:

The quick ratio is another liquidity ratio and it works the SAME as the current ratio, but you take out the effect of inventory. The reason for this is that for some industries, inventory can turn slower and you want to see what kind of "drag" the inventory has in your ability to pay your bills.

To do this calculation, you will subtract inventory from the ratio:

$$\frac{\text{Current Assets - Inventory}}{\text{Current Liabilities}}$$

Figure 16 Quick Ratio Calculation

Here you have a video helping to explain the quick ratio and its application (http://bit.ly/V1-4)

Figure 17 Video on Quick Ratio

Now, let us take a look to see if inventory affects Google and Amazon. First, Google:

Google (GOOG) 2018			Google (GOOG) 2017		
Current Assets	-	Inventory	Current Assets	-	Inventory
Current Liabilities			Current Liabilities		
$ 135,676.00	- $	1,107.00	$ 124,308.00	- $	749.00
$		34,620.00	$		24,183.00
		3.89			5.11

Figure 18 Quick Ratio Calculation for Google

For Google, you will be using the "Consolidated Balance Sheets" found on page 46 of the 10-k. You will pull the "Total current assets" for 2018 of $135,676, the "Inventory" of $1,107, and the "Total current liabilities" of $34,620. You will then pull the same data lines for 2017.

The current ratio for Google, we had calculated as 3.92, and the quick ratio for 2018 is 3.89. Therefore, inventory does not have a significant impact on the current ratio at all. Therefore, even if the inventory moved slowly, its impact will be relatively small.

Now, let us compare these results to Amazon:

Amazon (AMZN) 2018			Amazon (AMZN) 2017		
Current Assets	-	Inventory	Current Assets	-	Inventory
Current Liabilities			Current Liabilities		
$ 75,101.00	- $	17,174.00	$ 60,197.00	- $	16,047.00
$		68,391.00	$		57,883.00
		0.85			0.76

Figure 19 Quick Ratio Calculation for Amazon

For Amazon, you will be pulling data from the "Consolidated Balance Sheets" on page 39 of the 10-k. You will pull for 2018 the "Total current assets" line of $75,101, the "Inventories" line of $17,174, and the "Total current liabilities" of $68,391. You will then pull the same data lines for 2017.

The current ratio for Amazon was calculated as 1.10 for 2018, and our quick ratio for Amazon in 2018 is .85. This is a much bigger impact on Amazon's current ratio. Thus, if inventory is not turning quickly at Amazon, the impact to cash generation will be much bigger.

Now, what this tells us is that inventory has a bigger impact on liquidity at Amazon than it does at Google.

Accounts Receivable Turnover:

Accounts Receivable (A/R) Turnover is an important metric to calculate. The A/R Turnover shows you how often in a year you turn your accounts receivable into cash.

The calculation is conducted as follows:

$$\frac{Revenue}{Average\ Accounts\ Receivable}$$

Figure 20 A/R Turnover Calculation

In this calculation the revenue number is taken from the income statement and the average accounts receivable is taken from the balance sheet. In addition, you take the current year accounts receivable and the previous year's accounts receivable and add those numbers together and divide by two. For this book, this is the calculation, because a lot of analysts like to "smooth out" the accounts receivable balance by using an average. However, you may also find on the web that this can also be calculated without the average.

Here is a video to aid in learning about the Accounts Receivable Turnover ratio (http://bit.ly/V1-5)

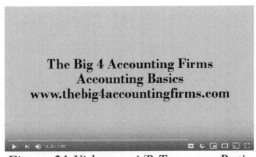

Figure 21 Video on A/R Turnover Ratio

Now, let us compare the data from Amazon and Google:

Amazon's 2018 results are:

			Amazon (AMZN) Numbers are in millions 2018	
2018 A/R	$	16,677.00	$	232,887.00
2017 A/R	$	13,164.00	$	14,920.50
2018 Avg	$	14,920.50		15.61

Figure 22 A/R Turnover Calculation for Amazon

For Amazon you will utilize both the "Consolidated Balance Sheets" on 37 of the 10-k and the "Consolidated Statements of Operations" on page 37 to pull the data for this calculation. You will pull from the "Consolidate Statements of Operations" the "Total net sales" $232,887 as the revenue numerator in the equation.

Then, you will use the "Consolidated Balance Sheets" on page 39 to pull the "Accounts receivable, net and other" for 2018 of $16,677 and the "Accounts receivable, net and other" for 2017 of $13,164. Add the $16,677 and the $13,164 and divide by 2 to get an average of $14,920.50.

The result of the A/R Turnover for Amazon is 15.61. This means accounts receivable turns into cash for Amazon 15.61 times in a year. We do not know if this is a respectable number until we build a trend for Amazon and/or compare this number to competitors.

Then, for Google in 2018:

			Google (GOOG) Numbers are in millions 2018
2018 A/R	$	20,838.00	$ 136,819.00
2017 A/R	$	18,336.00	$ 19,587.00
2018 Avg	$	19,587.00	6.99

Figure 23 A/R Turnover Calculation for Google

For Google you will utilize both the "Consolidated Balance Sheets" on 46 of the 10-k and the "Consolidated Statements of Income" on page 47 to pull the data for this calculation.

You will pull from the "Consolidate Statements of Income" the "Revenues" of $136,819 as the revenue numerator in the equation.

Then, you will use the "Consolidated Balance Sheets" on to pull the "Accounts receivable, net of allowance $674 and $729" for 2018 of $20,838 and the "Accounts receivable, net of allowance $674 and $729" for 2017 of $18,336. Add the $20,838 and the $18,336 and divide by 2 to get an average of $19,587.

The result of the A/R Turnover for Google is 6.99. This means accounts receivable turns into cash for Google 6.99 times in a year. We do not know if this is a respectable number until we build a trend for Google and/or compare this number to competitors.

As far as Amazon and Google perform for 2018, Amazon is performing better in turning their receivables into cash. From these calculations, we can see that Amazon turned its accounts receivable 15.61 times in 2018, and Google turned its accounts receivable 6.99 times.

Days Sales Outstanding:

Once you have the accounts receivable turnover you can now calculate the Days Sales Outstanding numbers. This will show how many days it takes, on average, to turn accounts receivable into cash. To do this you take 365 days in a year and divide it by the accounts receivable turnover number you just calculated.

Here is a video explaining this calculation (http://bit.ly/V1-6)

Figure 24 Video on Days Sales Outstanding (DSO)

Amazon (AMZN) Days Sales Outstanding	Google (GOOG) Days Sales Outstanding
365	365
15.61	6.99
23.38	52.25

Figure 25 DSO Google v. Amazon

Here the results show that it takes Amazon 23.38 days to turn their accounts receivable, and it takes Google 52.25 days to turn its accounts receivables. Amazon is performing better in this category, but there could be a reason that Google is taking longer and if you do not work for Google then the best place to start in finding the answer will be the 10-k. You would want to search through the document looking for any reference to accounts receivable to see what they say.

Inventory:

Inventory represents various different types of inventory. Inventory can represent items that are being held for sales, OR it could be inventory that represents replacement parts. For some industries, it is possible to turn inventory in 30-60 days, but for other industries you could have some inventory sitting around for longer. For example, in the wine and spirits industry, aging of whiskey could take 20 years. Thus, for that industry, inventory might not get turned into cash as quickly as other industries.

Inventory Turnover:

The inventory turnover calculation is calculating how many times in a year a company turns its inventory into cash. The calculation works like this:

$$\frac{\text{Cost of Goods Sold}}{\text{Average Inventory}}$$

Figure 26 Inventory Turnover Calculation

In this calculation, you will still use revenue from the Income Statement and you will use inventory from the balance sheet. In this case, we are using average inventory, just like the calculation was done previously with accounts receivable turnover. You do not have to do it that way, BUT, if the average inventory is significantly different than the actual inventory, it might be wise to "smooth" out the numbers using an average.

A video on calculating the inventory turnover ratio:

Figure 27 Video on Inventory Turnover Ratio Calculation

Let us see how Google and Amazon compare:

			Amazon (AMZN) Numbers are in millions 2018
2018 Inv	$	17,174.00	$ 139,156.00
2017 Inv	$	16,047.00	$ 16,610.50
2018 Avg	$	16,610.50	8.38
			Google (GOOG) Numbers are in millions 2018
2018 Inv	$	1,107.00	$ 59,549.00
2017 Inv	$	749.00	$ 928.00
2018 Avg	$	928.00	64.17

Figure 28 Inventory Turnover or Amazon and Google

For Amazon, you will be pulling data from the "Consolidated Balance Sheets" on page 39 and the "Consolidated Statements of Operations" on page 37. For Google, you will be pulling data from the "Consolidated Balance Sheets on page 46 and from the "Consolidated Statements of Income" on page 47.

For Amazon, you pull the "Cost of Sales" from the Consolidated Statements of Operations for $139,156. Then, from the Consolidated Balance Sheets, you pull the "Inventories" for 2018 of $17,174 and for 2017 of $16,047. Add the $17,174 to $16,047 and then divide by 2 and you get average inventories of $16,610.50. Plugging this data into the inventory turnover ratio you get a result that Amazon turns its inventory 8.38 times a year.

For Google, you will pull the "Cost of revenues" from the Consolidated Statements of Income for 2018, which is $59,549. Then, you will pull "Inventory" for 2018 of $1,107 and for 2017 of $749, add those numbers together and divide by 2 to get average inventory of $928. Plugging the data into the inventory turnover ratio you get a result of 64.17.

In these calculations you can see that for Amazon they can turn their inventory 8.38 times a year and Google can turn its inventory 64.60 times a year. In this metric, Google is performing better than Amazon.

Days in Inventory:

Now, we can also take the inventory turnover and turn it into a Days in Inventory calculation that tells us how many days, on average, it takes for these companies to turn their inventory into cash. You take 365 days in a year and divide that by the inventory turnover result to get the days.

Here is a video explaining this ratio (http://bit.ly/V1-7)

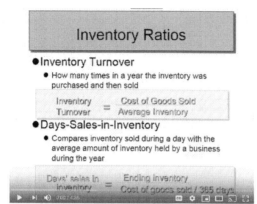

Figure 29 Video on Days in Inventory Ratio

Here are the results for Google and Amazon:

Amazon (AMZN) Days Inventory Outstanding	Google (GOOG) Days Inventory Outstanding
365	365
8.38	64.17
43.57	5.69

Figure 30 Google and Amazon Days in Inventory

Implications for your learning:

1. Understand the power of the ratios that can be derived from the balance sheet of your company

2. How you manage your cash is represented in many of the ratios from the balance sheet
3. The balance sheet ratios give you an idea of how efficiently you are managing your working capital

Topic 8: Balance Sheet – Liabilities

What are Liabilities?

Liabilities are the amounts of money owed to another party. One of the more common liabilities is Accounts Payable, and then you may also have long term liabilities that are often amounts that are owed to lending institutions for longer than a year.

Accounts Payable:

Accounts Payable will typically represent the amounts owed to suppliers.

Accounts Payable Turnover:

Accounts Payable turnover is a measure that looks at how quickly a company is using cash, not generating cash. The calculation looks like this:

$$\frac{\text{Cost of Goods Sold}}{\text{Average Accounts Payable}}$$

Figure 31 Accounts Payable Turnover

Cost of goods sold will be pulled from the income statement and the accounts payable will be pulled from the balance sheet. In this calculation you see an average used again because of a smoothing factor that may be important to you.

This video discusses the Accounts Payable Turnover ratio AND the Days Payable Outstanding (DPO) (http://bit.ly/V1-8)

Figure 32 Payables Turnover and DPO Video

If you look around the web for videos on this topic you may see some calculations using "payables on credit" instead of "cost of goods sold". If you were able to get that information about a company, that would be more accurate, BUT, most of the time, unless you have access to an accounts payable department in a company, you will have to use cost of goods sold instead.

Now, here are the calculations for Google and Amazon:

			Amazon (AMZN) Numbers are in millions 2018	
2018 A/P	$	38,192.00	$	139,156.00
2017 A/P	$	34,616.00	$	36,404.00
2018 Avg	$	36,404.00		3.82
			Google (GOOG) Numbers are in millions 2018	
2018 A/P	$	4,378.00	$	59,549.00
2017 A/P	$	3,137.00	$	3,757.50
2018 Avg	$	3,757.50		15.85

Figure 33 Google and Amazon A/P Turnover Calculation

For Amazon, you will be pulling data from the "Consolidated Balance Sheets" on page 39 and the "Consolidated Statements of Operations" on page 37. For Google, you will be pulling data from the "Consolidated Balance Sheets on page 46 and from the "Consolidated Statements of Income" on page 47.

For Amazon, you pull the "Cost of Sales" from the Consolidated Statements of Operations for $139,156. Then, from the Consolidated Balance Sheets, you pull the "Accounts Payable" for 2018 of $38,192 and for 2017 of $34,616. Add the $38,192 to $34,616 and then divide by 2 and you get average inventories of $36,404. Plugging this data into the inventory turnover ratio you get a result that Amazon turns its inventory 3.82 times a year.

For Google, you will pull the "Cost of revenues" from the Consolidated Statements of Income for 2018, which is $59,549. Then, you will pull "Accounts Payable" for 2018 of $4,378 and for 2017 of $3,137, add those numbers together and divide by 2 to get average inventory of $3,757.50. Plugging the data into the inventory turnover ratio you get a result of 15.85.

We see from the calculation that Amazon turns it Accounts Payable 3.82 times a year and Google turns 15.85 times a year. For this point in time, Amazon performs better because Accounts Payable is a "use" of cash.

Days Payables Outstanding:

Once you have calculated the accounts payable turnover you can then calculate a Days Payables Outstanding. You will use 365 days in a year and divide by the accounts payable turnover result.

Here are the results for Google and Amazon:

Amazon (AMZN) Days Payables Outstanding	Google (GOOG) Days Payables Outstanding
365	365
3.82	15.85
95.49	23.03

Figure 34 DPO Calculation for Google and Amazon

From this calculation, you can see that it takes Amazon 95.49 days to use the cash for accounts payable, and it takes Google 23.03 days to use cash for accounts payable.

Cash Conversion Cycle:

One of the interesting things you can assess in companies is their cash conversion cycle. To calculate the cash conversion cycle, you will add the days sales outstanding plus the days in inventory minus the day's payables outstanding.

Here is the calculation:

```
+ Days Sales Outstanding
+ Days in Inventory
 - Days Payables Outstanding

= Cash Conversion Cycle in Days
```

Figure 35 Cash Conversion Cycle Calculation

The reason that you have a "plus" before days sales outstanding and days in inventory is because these activities generate cash. The minus in front of days payables outstanding is because that activity uses cash.

Here is a supplemental video to aid your learning (http://bit.ly/V1-9)

Figure 36 Video on Cash Conversion Cycle (CCC)

Now, let us take a look at how this works for Amazon and Google:

	2018	
	Amazon	Google
+ Days Sales Outstanding	23.38	52.25
+ Days in Inventory	43.57	5.69
- Days Payables Outstanding	(95.49)	(23.03)
= Cash Conversion Cycle in Days	(28.53)	34.91

Figure 37 CCC Calculations for Amazon and Google

Let us breakdown these results. A negative number in the case of cash conversion cycle is actually a positive result. In the case of Amazon, the overall cash conversion cycle is a negative 28.53 days. Looking at the details we see that Amazon can generate cash in less than 30 days, but they can hold on to cash for over three months. They are generating cash way faster than they have to use money.

For Google, they are doing ok with their cash conversion cycle. They generate cash faster with inventory, but the generation of cash through accounts receivable is longer. But an overall cash conversion cycle of about a month is still good.

Debt to Assets Ratio

Another ratio that can be particularly useful to calculate is the debt to assets ratio. This ratio gives you an idea about the solvency of a company. Solvency means that in the long term, the company is viable, financially. Remember, the current ratio looks at current assets and current liabilities, looking at the short-term liquidity of being able to pay bills. But this ratio includes all the longer-term assets and liabilities so that you can determine if the company has a good chance of surviving in the long term.

Here is how the debt to assets ratio is calculated:

$$\frac{\text{Total Liabilities}}{\text{Total Assets}}$$

Figure 38 Debt to Assets Ratio

Here is a video that describes this ratio (http://bit.ly/V1-10)

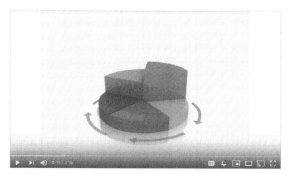

Figure 39 Debt to Asset Ratio Video

Now, let us see how much Amazon is leveraged through debt:

Amazon (AMZN)	
Numbers are in millions	
2018	2017
$ 119,099.00	$ 103,601.00
$ 162,648.00	$ 131,310.00
0.73	0.79

Figure 40 Debt to Assets Calculation for Amazon

For Amazon, you will be pulling data from the "Consolidated Balance Sheets" on page 39 of the 10-k. Then, for 2018, you pull the "Total assets" of $162,648 and you will have to "back into" the total liabilities number. To calculate total liabilities, you will add the "Total current liabilities" of $68,391, plus the "Long-term debt" of $23,495, and add the "Other long-term liabilities" of $27,213 to get a total liabilities number of $119,099.

The goal of the debt to assets ratio is that it is less than 1. The smaller number is the better number. In Amazon's case, the ratio is less than 1. What this means is that the company is leveraged by debt in 2018 by 73% and the rest is financed by equity.

Now, let us take a look at Google:

Google (GOOG)		
Numbers are in millions		
	2018	2017
$	55,164.00	$ 44,793.00
$	232,792.00	$ 197,295.00
	0.24	0.23

Figure 41 Debt to Assets Calculation for Google

For Google, you will be using the "Consolidated Balance Sheets" on page 46 of the 10-k. For 2018 for Google, you will pull the "Total assets" amount of $232,792. Then, you will pull the "Total liabilities" number of $55,164.

For Google, the ratio calculates to be less than 1 as well. For Google, the company is leveraged, or financed, by debt in 2018 is 24% and the rest is financed by equity.

Implications for your learning:

1. Understand the power of the ratios that can be derived from the balance sheet of your company
2. How you manage your cash is represented in many of the ratios from the balance sheet

3. The cash conversion cycle ratio gives you a good idea of how well you are managing your working capital and cash.
4. Debt to Assets helps you to know the long-term viability of your company

Topic 9: Balance Sheet – Equity

What is Equity?

The equity section of a balance sheet shows how much equity is being built up in the business from the operations of the business or through stock sales. You will want to look at the Consolidated Balance Sheets for Google on page 46 of their 10-k, and look at the Consolidated Balance Sheets for Amazon on page 39 of their 10-k.

If your company is publicly traded, then you will have equity generated through the sale of stock. If you are not publicly traded, this type of equity will not be present in the equity section of your balance sheet.

If your company is not publicly traded, then your equity will be built through the operations of the business. One thing to note about this is the relationship between the income statement and the balance sheet.

Every month, the income statement NET profit or loss is moved to the retained earnings account in the equity section of the balance sheet. Thus, every revenue account, every cost of goods sold account, and every expense account balance is reduced to a ZERO so that the next month's income statement can account for the current month's data.

Thus, if you have $100,000 in revenue this month, that $100,000 will be moved to Retained Earnings and the next month will start with a zero balance in the revenue accounts. The same process will happen with all of the expense accounts.

Here is a visual representation of this process:

Figure 42 Relationship of P&L to Retained Earnings

Now, here is another way to look at the balance sheet. When you look at a balance sheet, there is always three different sections:

Assets

Liabilities

Equity

You will notice, on any balance sheet, that the Assets total amount will equal the liabilities total amount PLUS the equity total amount. This is what is known as the "accounting equation". And it is why the Balance Sheet must "balance".

For example, in looking at Amazon's 2018 balance sheet, the total liabilities equal $119,099 and the equity balance is $43,549 and those added together equal $162,648. That number is the SAME as the total assets for Amazon. But, more importantly, look at the percentage of stock versus financing versus retained earnings for Google:

	2018	% of Total Liabilities	% of Total Libailities and Equity
Current Liabilities	34,620.00	63%	15%
Long Term Debt	20,544.00	37%	9%
Total Liabilties	55,164.00		24%
		% of Total Equity	
Stock	45,049.00	25%	19%
Retained Earnings	134,885.00	76%	58%
Total Equity	177,628.00		76%
Total Liabilities and Equity	232,792.00		

Figure 43 Analysis of Google Balance Sheet

This shows a nice balance for Google. The current liabilities are the bigger percentage of liabilities. Plus, most of Google's equity is being generated through operations. Even when you look at overall contribution to the total liabilities and equity, retained earnings is contributing more than 50%.

Implications for your learning:

1. Equity should mostly come from your operations
2. Equity from operations comes onto the balance each month after the income statement is closed

Topic 10: Cash Flow

Cash is King.

Understanding how cash flows through an organization is important. Cash is the life blood of a company and thus knowing how quickly the company generates cash and how they use cash is essential to managing the business.

In Amazon's 10-k, you will want to look at the "Consolidated Statements of Cash Flows" on page 36. In Google's 10-k, you will want to look at the "Consolidated Statements of Cash Flows" on page 50.

What does a cash flow statement tell you?

A cash flow statement tells you how money is generated and used through operations, investing, and financing.

Cash generated (or used) from operating activities.

If you examine the cash flow statement for Amazon on Page 36 of the 10-k for 2018, you will see that operations generated cash of $30,723,000,000. This money is the generation of cash through managing accounts receivable, inventory, and accounts payable. There is also a line for unearned revenue that was discussed in Topic 2.

In addition, it is important to note that there is a line called "Depreciation of property and equipment and other amortization, including capitalized content costs". In Topic 5, depreciation was noted as being a NON-CASH activity, meaning that there was no exchange of cash for depreciation. In other words, there was no check written to a government agency for depreciation you will add the depreciation back to the cash balance on the cash flow statement.

Cash generated (or used) from investing activities. Investing activities will generally be investments that companies make into their operations or there will be investments in securities.

If you examine the cash flow statement for Amazon on Page 36 of the 10-k for 2018 there are purchases of property and equipment and there are sales and purchases of marketable securities. On page 50 of the Google 10-k you see the same pattern of purchases and sales.

Cash generated (or used) from financing activities.

If you examine the cash flow statement for Amazon on Page 36 of the 10-k for 2018, you see that the Amazon is repaying long-term debt and other obligations. In addition, companies can issue debt for the public to invest in and this would be classified as proceeds to the company.

For Google, on page 50 of the 10-k you see where debt has been issued to the public, and they are paying long term debt and they are listing common stock uses of cash and generation of cash.

Free Cash Flow.

Free cash flow is the money that is free from capital expenditures. Thus, if you look at the cash flow statement and you take the cash flow from operations (i.e., Amazon had cash generated from operations of $30,723 in 2018) and subtract the capital expenditures (in this case in the cash flow for Amazon in 2018 in the "investing" section you have $(13,427) as the number) – then your free cash flow is $17,296. That free cash flow can then be used on many different kinds of projects. That money can be used to pay dividends, it can be turned into more investments into equipment, or other capital projects.

Implications for your learning:

1. Understand the three sections of the cash flow statement – cash flow from operations, investing, and financing
2. Free cash flow is a measure of seeing how much free cash you after paying for capital expenditures

Topic 11: Working Capital Management

What is working capital?

When someone refers to working capital, they are referring to the effective management of current assets of the business and your current liabilities. The current assets you will typically see on the balance sheet are cash, accounts receivable, inventory and the current liability of Accounts Payable.

Essentially, you want to think of working capital as the cash that helps you keep the operations running. Thus, you are focusing on turning your inventory and accounts receivable into cash as quickly as possible and holding onto your cash in accounts payable for as long as you can.

How to manage accounts receivable.

To manage accounts receivable there are several things that you can do to ensure that accounts receivable is managed efficiently.

Invoicing customers: A common way to deal with customers is to invoice them for products or services. One of the essential elements of invoicing customers is knowing the customer's credit history. To do this, you would want to consider having a credit application and run a business credit report. Thus, upfront, before you sell to someone or to a company, if the invoice totals are going to be substantial to you, then you want to know how well they have paid their bills in the past.

In addition to the upfront decision of IF you will be extending credit to customers, on the back end you want to keep track of how your accounts receivable is aging. In other words, if you extend credit terms to a customer that the customer can pay their invoice in 30 days, then you want to watch and see if invoices are consistently going beyond the 30 days' timeframe to be paid.

In most accounting software that exists today an accounts receivable aging report is a typical type of report that can be run any time. The report will list all of the open invoices, usually grouped by customer, and showing the due dates and amounts of the invoices. In addition, the report can group invoices by "current", meaning that the invoice is currently within the terms that you have granted the customer. Another bucket could be invoices that are beyond the 30 days credit terms you have granted the customer, but still within 60 days, etc. Here is an example of what a report like this may look like:

Date of report: 07/26/2019

Customer	Invoice Number	Amount	Invoice Date	Current	>30 days	>60 Days	>120 Days
ABC Co	1234	$ 5,000.00	7/10/2019	$5,000.00			
	1236	$ 6,250.00	2/14/2019				$6,250.00
XYZ Co	1235	$ 4,000.00	6/30/2019	$4,000.00			
	1237	$ 1,250.00	5/1/2019			$1,250.00	
	1238	$ 3,450.00	4/15/2019			$3,450.00	
Totals		$19,950.00		$9,000.00		$4,700.00	$6,250.00

Figure 44 A Sample Accounts Receivable Aging Report

Thus, as a business owner you want to keep an eye on, or have someone following up on, any invoice that is in the buckets other than "current".

Other billing scenarios: Not all information technology businesses would necessarily invoice customers. With the advent of credit cards and online buying, many businesses today immediately charge a customer's credit card. With a merchant services account, you can bill a credit card or allow a customer to pay by credit card, and you can get the cash quickly, usually within a day or two. Many of the merchant services companies out there a customer can send a direct ACH (Automated Clearing House) bank-to-bank transfer and the money can come into your bank account usually within five days.

In these situations, the invoices or the billing will not be open long. Plus, if you have a retail presence in a brick and mortar store, there would be no invoicing of a customer at all.

How to manage accounts payable.

In software systems a company can keep track of their open invoices. Just like invoices to customers, you can keep track of the invoices from suppliers and run reports showing the aging of these documents. Thus, you want to negotiate good terms for your company on supplier invoices.

Date of report: 07/26/2019

Customer	Invoice Number	Amount	Invoice Date	Current	>30 days	>60 Days	>120 Days
ABC Supplier	10345	$ 4,000.00	2/14/2019				$4,000.00
	9456	$ 6,000.00	7/10/2019	$6,000.00			
XYZ Supplier	1853	$ 3,000.00	4/12/2019			$3,000.00	
	1734	$ 1,200.00	5/1/2019		$1,200.00		
	1436	$ 3,000.00	6/28/2019	$3,000.00			
Totals		$17,200.00		$9,000.00	$1,200.00	$3,000.00	$4,000.00

Figure 45 A/P Aging

One of the ways you manage the supplier invoices is through incentives for paying early. Thus, one way to measure effectiveness of Accounts Payable is to measure discounts lost. For instance, a supplier may give you credit terms of paying invoice in 30 days, BUT, the same supplier may give you an incentive to pay that invoice early. For example, it could be that the supplier gives you a 2% discount to pay the invoice within 15 days.

Consider this example: If you have terms of 2% 15 days, net 30 and you have an invoice that the supplier has sent you for $10,000. If you pay the invoice on the 14th day, you would only pay $9,800, not $10,000. However, after the 15th day, you would be paying $10,000.

Thus, if you paid the invoice on day 30, you would have a discount lost of $200. Software today can keep track of the discounts lost and this is a direct reflection of how well a company manages the outflow, or usage, of cash.

How to manage inventory.

Managing inventory is all about the turnover. One of the best ways to keep track of turnover is to calculate a turnover ratio for each and every part or type of product.

Companies should have an inventory system where you can pull cost of goods sold for individual part numbers as well as the inventory on hand for those part numbers. This is something that must be reviewed on a regular basis, because you can easily spot items that are languishing in your inventory. Purchasing agents sometimes are lured by a "good deal" when there is no demand for that product. Or, you could have spare parts that go to a finished good that you no longer manufacture. Even if you cannot sell those parts, you want to free up space and get whatever money you can for those parts if they cannot be used in any other goods you produce.

Therefore, you are looking for obsolete products, so that you can get whatever cash you can for letting them go, write them off, or repurpose these products.

Here is a video about obsolete inventory – the information part of the video is about 30 minutes long, but valuable information (http://bit.ly/V1-11)

Figure 46 Video about obsolete inventory

How to manage cash.

The important thing about cash is that you will not have cash generally lying around in a business. Thus, in managing cash you are setting targets for how much cash you will keep on hand and how much cash you will be willing to reinvest into the company.

Unless you actually have a retail component to your business, it is likely that you will not have a need for any cash lying around, so it is best that your cash stay at the bank for safeguarding. If you do not have a retail presence you want to make sure that your inventory and accounts receivable are turning into cash as quickly as possible.

But, on the off chance that you do have cash actually coming into your business, then it is a god idea to pay attention to the internal controls' topic of the book.

One last thing – you will want to determine how much cash you want to have on hand and how much you earmark for investing back into your business. Early on in business development, you may have to use all of your cash to keep up with startup bills, but if you have a sound business idea in the technology arena, you will be able to keep a certain amount of cash on hand – the free cash flow – that will give you the ability to invest in yourself, pay bills, or acquire a business. Cash can give you a tremendous amount of corporate leverage!

Here is a great video about all of these topics and why it is important to your cash flow (http://bit.ly/V1-13)

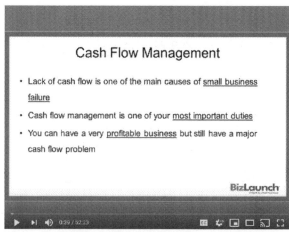

Figure 47 Cash Flow Management Video

Implications for your learning:

1. Keep an eye on accounts receivable and inventory to make sure cash is coming into the business
2. Utilize terms from suppliers as long as you can – if you can negotiate favorable terms that go at least 30-60 days is ideal

Topic 12: Budgeting

What is budgeting?

Budgeting is a process by which a person or group of people forecast business activity over a period of time. Many budgets will be over a period of a fiscal year.

What is a static budget?

Basically, a static budget, once it is approved, never changes during the year. For example, let us say that last year your small business hired 12 new employees. Each of these new employees get an office365 subscription as part of their employment and a new Dell laptop. The office365 subscription cost is $110 a year and a new surface pro that you are estimated to be $1,500 each, which include accessories.

A big question you have is, are you going to hire the same amount of people next year? Maybe the plan is you will be hiring another 12, or you are anticipating growth of approximately 25% in your business, so you plan on hiring 15 people (that is 12 times 1.25).

Thus, 15 new people next year, at a cost of $1,610 each would give you an annual budget of $24,150.

Now, the next question is how do you spread that over your fiscal year of twelve months? For some departments, you may spread the $24,150 evenly over 12 months. You would then take the $24,150 and divide by 12 and you would have a monthly budget of $2,012.50.

For some departments this could really be arbitrary and not really reflect the true fluctuation of hiring. Maybe, in your analysis, you see that you hire less people in the first quarter, and then you start ramping up in the second quarter and your highest quarters of hiring are in quarters three and four.

Let us say that your data tells you that you tend to hire in this pattern (using the 12 hires as the baseline):

Quarter 1 = 2 hires

Quarter 2 = 2 hires

Quarter 3 = 4 hires

Quarter 4 = 4 hires

Then you can produce a number that more reflects this hiring pattern for your budget. Thus, in quarters one and two you would be hiring 16.67% of the 15 people, and we round that up to 3 people hired.

In quarter three and four then you would base your hiring on 33.33% of the 15 hires rounding up to five hires in those quarters. Here would be the hiring pattern:

Quarter 1 = 3 hires

Quarter 2 = 3 hires

Quarter 3 = 5 hires

Quarter 4 = 5 hires

Then, of course, you still have to drill down to how many people you think you will hire each month. With the 6 hires on the first 6 months, you can assume one hire per month. With the 10 hires in the last half of the year, you may hire two each month for the first four months, and then one each month at the end of the year.

The big deal here is that you have to determine the activity that drives the expense AND you have to document your assumptions. In this case, the technology expense is DRIVEN by the new hires. Thus, how much you spend on technology will depend on the estimate of the new hires that you are planning for the year. Plus, you can see from our previous conversation about this in what assumptions we are making in WHEN the hires will be made. Knowing this information helps you to explain variances.

How do you interpret and explain budget variances?

Once you establish a budget, you will eventually have to explain variances. Let's assume we have the following budget for the first quarter of the year for outfitting new hires with technology (remember, we are assuming ONE hire each month based on a $24,150 yearly budget amount):

	Month 1		Month 2		Month 3	
	Budget	Actual	Budget	Actual	Budget	Actual
Hiring	1	2	1		1	
Technology	$1,610.00	$3,500.00	$1,610.00		$1,610.00	

Assumptions:
Hiring one person each month in the first quarter, plus 25% growth
Assuming a total cost of $1,610 per hire
Assuming no significant change in the costs over the year

Figure 48 Budget Example

Now, you can see that the budget was $1,610.00, but the actual was $3,500.00. This gives a variance for the first month of $1,890.00. Intuitively, you have spent MORE than what you BUDGETED; therefore, this is a negative variance (or unfavorable variance). It is preferable that you use "unfavorable" because when you use the word "negative", you might start to think of "minus", which can get you into the wrong thinking pattern of math.

So, how do you explain this? Well one part of the explanation here is going to be regarding the "volume" of hiring – the cost "driver", or activity, we have identified in the budgeting process. We had budgeted for only ONE hire in the first month, but we actually hired TWO.

However, there is also a cost factor here. Our budget is based on $1,610.00 as a cost per hire. Thus, we would have anticipated a cost of $3,220.00 instead of $3,500.00. Thus, costs are increasing, it appears, and we will need to explain why. Maybe it is because our original assumption of a cost of $1,500 was not accurate for a surface pro, or the costs of accessories has gone up for some reason. Either way, you would explain this variance from an activity perspective AND a cost perspective.

You can also break out this variance if $1,890.00 into what amount is attributed to the extra person that has been hired and break out the part that is attributed to the increase in costs.

In this case, the actual quantity of 2 minus the budgeted quantity of 1 will equal 1. And we multiply that by the cost we had budgeted of $1,610. Thus, the volume variance is $1,610.

Then, in the case of the overall costs, we had budgeted $1,610 minus the actual cost of $1,750 gives us $140 times the actual number of hires. Therefore, 2 times $140 = $280.

The volume variance of $1,610 (unfavorable), plus the price variance of $280 (unfavorable), gives us a total unfavorable variance of $1,890. To check our math, the amount spent in total of $3,500 - $1,610 of the original budgeted monthly amount gives us a difference of $1,890. The math works!

You can also conclude that the biggest driver behind the budget variance is the volume of new hires.

When do you need to adjust a static budget?

There are times that you may want to adjust a static budget during the year. There are a few things you want to think about.

First, you do not want to do this too often, because the budget can quickly lose the meaning of its purpose. Part of the financial intelligence of managers is that you have to use your budget as an educational tool for yourself to learn about the nuances and influences that cause your budget to ebb and flow. Thus, if you hire more people in this technology budge than what you had anticipated, it is worth having a discussion with human resources and other managers in the company or department to work on how to more accurately forecast hiring.

Secondly, a year is a long time. Costs and plans can shift significantly because business is taking off quicker than expected, or the economy is slowing more than expected, or some other factor that you could not have predicted. For instance, sometimes there is a raw material costs that starts to shoot up in price. Gasoline and other commodities can have huge fluctuations at times. If these costs are driving changes in costs, you may have to adjust your budget. At best, a budget should be reworked, if you are going to do that, on a semi-annual basis. At worst, you would want to adjust the budget quarterly.

How could you use a flexible budget?

One of the ways to deal with fluctuations like we have been discussing is to use a flexible budget. Remember back when we first talked about a budget, we assumed a 25% growth? Well, that is only one scenario.

With a flexible budget, you could environment several scenarios. For example, you could anticipate one scenario being 25% lower than the year before. Thus, if we had hired 12 people, our 25% lower budget would anticipate 9 hires (12 times .75 = 9).

We could still have our 25% better scenario, as scenario two, that assumes we would hire 15 (12 times 1.25 = 15).

And, we could have an even better scenario of that we double our hiring in a best-case scenario. Thus, 12 hires times 2 would be 24 hires in the budget.

Assuming that the cost of each hire, in terms of the technology cost would not change, only the volume changes, because perhaps that is the biggest drive of costs that we have seen over time.

In this flexible budget line item then, you would have three levels to compare to: 9 hires, 15 hires, and 24 hires – each of these broken down into the monthly split. Thus, in the case of our actual budget being 2 hires for the first month, using the original budget might be fine. However, as the year progresses, you may see you are more on track for the 24 hires, so you may go to that budget to explain variances sooner rather than later.

The advantage of budgeting like this is that you do not have to spend a lot of time developing a new budget if you need to make adjustments at the halfway point of the year. Essentially, the only task you would be doing then is validating assumption on the 24 hires, which takes a lot less time than completely developing a new budget.

Implications for your learning:

1. Budgets can take time to develop

2. Most companies use static budgets, but learning how to use a flexible budget can be useful to you

3. Explaining variances is important as a business owner or as a manager

4. Documenting your assumptions will be critical in being able to explain variances

Topic 13: Return on Investment

What is return on investment?

Return on investment is a process by which a company models out different opportunities, or projects, and how that investment of money will generate cash flow or save money.

At the basic level, a return on investment model seeks to find out what kind of return you are getting on your money. For example, a business may invest some of their cash into a certificate of deposit. Maybe you invest $10,000 and you earn 2% on that money in one year. Your "return" is the 2%. Now, if the money is earning interest quarterly, the annualized rate of return will be a little more than 2%, because you are earning interest on interest.

However, you get the idea. A company can invest money in all sorts of investment opportunities. For example, a company could decide to invest money in acquiring another business. A company could decide they need to upgrade their technology platforms, like investing in software or hardware. Or a company could invest in another building for a server farm.

It is easy to understand that an investment is going to require putting up cash/money for that investment. However, the other part of this, determining what earning or savings will be generated because of that outlay of money can be the harder part of the equation. Thus, our equation looks like this:

$$\frac{\text{Net Income}}{\text{Investment}}$$

Figure 49 ROI Calculation Formula

The numerator can be the net income earned on the investment, or the cash flow earned on the investment, or the cash savings on the investment. This also does not mean that you would ignore decision criteria that is hard to quantify in cash earnings or savings, because, you want to identify those variables as well.

Thus, when building a return on investment model, you want to think through all of the possible variables, costs, or savings that could be present as you analyze the situation.

For example, if you are a technology company protecting the data of corporations in cloud services, it would be hard to predict the cost of any one litigation case if you were to have a data breach. However, would there be a way that the cost could be recouped over time in subscription fees for your cloud services, AND you do not want to ignore the potential cost in the courts, or loss of customers, if you did have a data breach.

Here is a video that talks about the basics of return on investment (ROI) (http://bit.ly/V1-14)

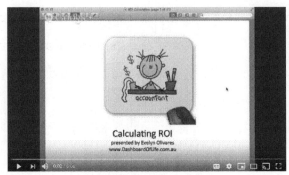

Figure 50 ROI Video

Let us consider an example. Suppose that you are a company that has inventory and you had to make a large $1.3 million dollar write off of inventory one year because you have a problem seeing the aging of your inventory. Your current software does not give you any visual aids in analyze inventory aging.

If a solution were to cost you $500,000, to ensure that you no longer had large inventory write offs like that, would you do it? The answer may likely be yes, because for an outlay of $500K, you can save a write off AND, if you have a tool to see the aging, you might be able to sell that inventory sooner, thus adding to your cash flow. Even if you estimate you could turn 70% of that inventory into a sale, because of the viability of the aging, then your cash flow could be $910,000 (1.3M times 70%). The return on the investment would be 182% ($910,000 / $500,000), this give you 1.82 times 100 = 182%.

That is a nice return!

The real key for doing any return on investment modeling is you want to be sure to:

1. Identify the variables that are important to the project
2. Identify how much it will cost
3. Identify any cash flows or cash savings in any way possible
4. Identify variables that are hard to quantify in terms of money, but are nonetheless important
5. DOCUMENT ALL OF YOUR ASSUMPTIONS

Every time a model like this is built, you want to learn from what you decided. You want to ensure that you have a way of following up to make sure you can track the actual cost of the project/investment, track the actual cash inflows or savings, so that over time you can solidify how you develop these models and make decisions.

Another important aspect to this is an ROI model does not assess risk. Thus, when considering a possible project, you will not be alone in doing this analysis. There are many people and departments that will be involved in the decision.

The important thing, as far as this book is concerned, is for you to start thinking about – what would be the essential elements that you think would be involved in buying new software, hardware or technology and how would you justify the purchase. An ROI model is one thing that you can use in building a case for the purchase/investment.

Implications for your learning:

1. Return on investment decisions are based on factor that you can generate cash flow or save money

2. You will also have to identify variables that may be difficult to estimate a cost, or savings – such as risk factors like avoiding lawsuits

3. Creating documentation of assumptions is crucial in return on investment case development

4. Working with other departments can increase your success in investment decisions, so that no stone is left unturned in identifying risks and benefits

Topic 14: Internal Controls

What are Internal Controls?

Internal controls are the processes procedures that a company uses to ensure that assets are protected in an organization from theft, fraud, and other abuses.

There are several standard considerations every business should consider when it comes to internal controls. In this section we will first talk about internal controls that would apply to an IT business or IT department.

Preventive Controls:

There are controls that are implemented to attempt to prevent fraud or loss from happening up front.

Segregation of Duties:

Segregation of duties is the ability to separate functions by distance, time, or people. For instance, if the same person processes purchase orders and processes invoices then it would make it much easier for an employee to set themselves up as a vendor and pay themselves.

In order to prevent this scenario, often, what larger companies will do is separate the department that processes purchase orders from the department that processes invoices for suppliers.

Here is a video that illustrates this idea in more detail (http://bit.ly/V1-15)

Figure 51 Video on Segregation of Duties

Pre-approvals:

Pre-approved transactions usually require a signature of an authorized individual. Or, in some cases, if the amount is above a certain threshold then the transaction may require two signatures. For some companies that could be a threshold of $5,000, or $25,000 or $100,000. Each company will have to determine what that threshold is for itself.

Now, even though there are two signatures, it does not mean that fraud could not happen. Individuals who have signature authority need to be trained on the responsibilities of those signatures. If a person is not clear that the signature represents that you fully understand why the purchase needs to be made, or that there is a valid business reason for the expense, ignorance could land you in jail.

In addition, the owner of a business should always sign checks, and certain thresholds of payments should always require two signatures.

Locks:

Sometimes a company has inventory on hand, or other items on hand, that could be of significant value, or valued by employees. For example, at Starbucks warehouses, they have to have a locked safe for the "free cup of coffee" coupons that they can give out in the retail stores. The reason for that is because employees could steal them otherwise and give them to friends.

Or, consider the fact that if an employee works for Microsoft, back when they had disks that implemented the software, these disks did not cost a lot. In fact, employees could get software for less than $50 in a lot of cases. Thus, in making sure that inventory did not just walk out the door in a person's coat or backpack, you had to have retail inventory control procedures in place.

Not everything can be locked up. For instance, a lot of companies have inventory that people may want at home.

In an IT organization, this could be thumb drives, computer drives, and other equipment. Not everything can be under lock and key, so you have to think about how you will ensure that your inventory does not get stolen. Even in a warehouse of computer equipment, you could have everything bar coded and have beepers sound off if the material moves beyond a certain boundary that the equipment should not cross.

Detective Controls:

These are controls that attempt to identify issues after the fact. These are often called "reconciliation" activities.

Surprise/Regular Counts:

A surprise count, or regularly scheduled count, can help to ensure that inventory is handled appropriately. For an IT company or department, keeping track of asset tags is a way of doing this and making those surprise counts or audits of inventory can be an effective way of keeping track of these assets.

In the case of a retail store, you will also need controls around the cash register. If you are a technology company that has a retail presence, you will want to make sure that you have tight controls of cash in the cash register. This can include the person that runs the register, and the person that does the count should be separate people.

Here is a video discussing a surprise count that can be applied to more than just cash, you can apply the strategy to all kinds of inventory as well (http://bit.ly/V1-16)

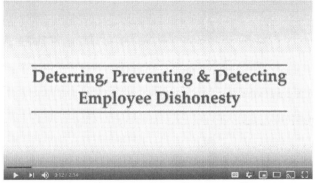

Figure 52 Video about Surprise Counts

Reconciliations:

Reconciliations can be of bank accounts or inventory. For instance, if you know that you have so many computer assets, when you do your count, you will need to reconcile the differences. If you have 500 computer assets in your organization, and you do an annual count and there are on 450, you will need to reconcile the missing 50 assets and have the ability to find those assets, or explain why they are not available for the count.

Audits:

Audits are a way of making sure that defined procedures and processes are updated and followed. For example, a company would want to identify the process and procedure for counting your computer assets every year. This is what is called a standard operating procedure. The document should include things like:

How is the asset tagging done?
Where is the main list of asset tags?

What happens if the count is off?

Who is responsible for tags? Or the count?

When does the count occur? Is it regular and random?

What happens when certain assets get to a certain age?

What documentation is required for the counting if the assets?

When you document these and other questions about your process and procedure, then someone can come along later and review that process and make sure that everything is working like you say it does. The person conducting the audit should not be in your same department, or it can be an external audit team that does this important review for you.

What can a small business do to protect itself?

The challenges for audit controls can be harder for a business that is small. When it comes to segregation of duties, for example, and you only have three individuals in the office, you can be hard pressed to separate duties. However, here is a great video on how small businesses can address this important success factor of implementing internal controls (http://bit.ly/V1-17)

Figure 53 Video on Small Business Internal Controls

The Impact of Sarbanes-Oxley:

The Sarbanes-Oxley (SOX) legislation was enacted after the collapse of Enron.

One requirement of SOX is the controls that now have to be implemented around the use of Excel. Companies have to determine what level of financial impact they want to avoid. For example, a company may decide that any Excel file that contains financial information that could impact the financial statements, or financial notes, by $50,000 positively or negatively will need to have controls implemented.

The same idea as presented earlier in this topic will apply, you can have preventive controls and detective controls. Here is a video outlining the background of this important legislation (http://bit.ly/V1-18)

Figure 54 Sarbanes-Oxley Video

Excel File Password Protection:

For example, a preventive control is to have password protection on a file. There are several different options on how to protect a file, and you can see how to do this on this video (be aware that this video is based on Excel 2016, if you have older versions, you may have to search the web for a more appropriate video):

http://bit.ly/V1-19

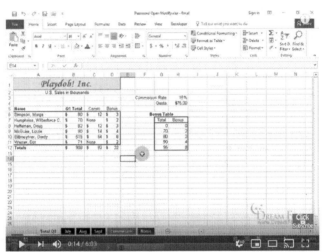

Figure 55 How to set Excel file passwords video

Password Protection of Cells in Excel Worksheets:

Another way of protecting information in a workbook is to learn how to protect cells in worksheets in Excel. For example, if you have formulas in worksheets, then you may want to consider protecting them so that a user cannot overwrite the formulas accidentally.

Here is a video that shows you how you can set up cell protection in an Excel worksheet (remember, this is Excel 2016, so if you have a different version you will need to do your own search on the web):

http://bit.ly/V1-20

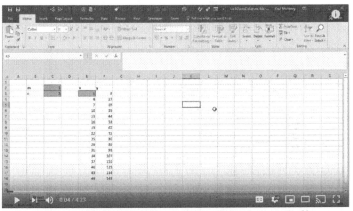

Figure 56 Video Excel 2016 Protecting Cells

Using Data Validation in Excel to Reduce Input Errors:

Another way of protecting information in a workbook is to utilize the data validation features of Excel. Data validation cuts down on input errors and can be applied to an Excel spreadsheet in a lot of different ways.

Here is a video that shows you how to do data validation: http://bit.ly/V1-21

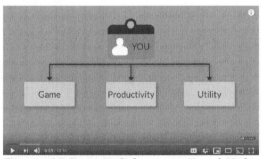

Figure 57 Data Validation in Excel Video

In and IT department, or IT company, there can be any kind of financial information that is tracked in Excel. Accounting software today may not handle all of the tracking necessary, or calculations necessary, to produce financial statements. The reason for this is because of the multi-national complexity of a lot of organizations today. Plus, if you start a company, often, your infrastructure and support function do not always keep up with the sales growth and expansion of the company.

Using an Accountant or Accounting Department:

If you are starting a company, or if your company has an accounting department, utilize the accounting resources to help you in developing these spreadsheet controls.

Implications for your learning:

1. Internal controls can be more difficult to implement in a small business, but you must figure out a way

2. Internal controls are a reflection of your ability to run a business with integrity

3. Excel still contains financial information, so learning how to protect that data is important

Topic 15: Contractors vs. Employees

In many businesses, you will have both types of workers, contract, and employee. This is true of technology departments, whether you are part of a technology company or not. Regardless of industry, if there is an IT department, you will use a mixture of employees and contractors to do the work of the IT department.

Why is this a common challenge for IT departments or businesses?

The reason this is common is because there are two distinct types of work in an IT department or company. The types of work are: "Support" work and "Project/Development" work.

In addition, IT leadership will look at their budgets in terms of "soft money" and "hard money". What does this mean?

An IT leader will look at "hard money" as being the expenses that impact the operating expenses of the profit and loss statement. "Soft money" is the capitalized money that goes into long-term projects that get expensed over a longer period of time.

Thus, support activities tend to be handled by full-time employees because these are the day-to-day activities of the IT department and there will always be steady amount of support work that has to be done in the organization.

However, larger, more expensive projects tend to be done with a mix of full-time employees and consulting support. Typically, this is because IT department leaders and managers tend to think of consulting services to be more expensive by the hour.

However, is this true? Let us examine what might go into this analysis.

For example, you might have an IT technical consultant that you are being charged $100 an hour. At first glance, this amount may seem like a really steep price to pay. Because, typically, a manager might look at this number and look at an equivalent job in your organization and you are spending $50 an hour for a person that earns a salary of $100,000 in your office.

We arrive at the $50 per hour by taking $100,000 and dividing by 2,000 hours in a year (this number is derived by assuming a person takes two weeks off a year and 40 hours of work for each of 50 weeks). However, looking at JUST the salary is not taking into account all of the costs of the employee.

For example, the costs of the employee include benefits (i.e., 401-k matches by the company, health benefits paid by the company, and the company Social Security and Medicare funds that are paid).

Thus, for our employee that makes $100,000 a year, if the company also pays $5,000 a month in matching funds for the 401-k, and pays $3,000 a month for health insurance for the employee and family, and there are company paid taxes of $7,650 a year in Social Security and Medicare taxes. So, let us see where we are now with the hourly wage of the employee.

Employee Salary	$100,000.00
Employer Paid: 401-k Matching Funds $5,000 * 12	$ 60,000.00
Employer Paid: Benefits $3,000 * 12	$ 36,000.00
Employer Paid: Social Security and Medicare	$ 7,650.00
TOTAL	$203,650.00

Figure 58 Employee versus Contractor

Then, the $203,650 divided by 2,000 hours in a year you get $102 per hour. Compared to the consultant for $100 an hour, then these two individuals cost just about the same amount of money per hour.

What does this mean to you as an IT manager?

Based on these calculations, an IT manager should have a list of internal human resources in the IT department and their actual cost per hour. It might even be a good idea to have the average cost by type of job or job title.

Implications for your learning:

1. It is very possible that an IT department will need to utilize contract employees for the fluctuating demands of projects

2. An IT manager and IT business owners need to understand how hard and soft money impacts the business and the financial statement

APPENDICES

Appendix A: Google and Amazon Financial Comparison

2018 Ratios

	Ratio	Amazon	Google
Profitability	Grosss Profit Margin	0.40	0.56
	Net Profit Margin	0.04	0.22
Liquidity	Current Ratio	1.10	3.92
	Quick Ratio	0.85	3.89
Solvency	Debt to Assets	0.73	0.24
Activity/Efficiency Ratios	A/R Turnover	15.61	6.99
	Days Sales Outstanding	23.38	52.25
	Inventory Turnover	8.38	64.17
	Days in Inventory	43.57	5.69
	A/P Turnover	3.82	15.85
	Days Payables Outstanding	95.49	23.03
	Cash Conversion Cycle	(28.53)	34.91
EBITDA		$27,762.00	$34,485.00
Free Cash Flow		$17,296.00	$22,842.00

Appendix B: Index

Made in the USA
Middletown, DE
04 January 2020